She Persisted

13 American Women Who Changed the World

I have never had to face anything that could overwhelm the native optimism and stubborn perseverance I was blessed with."

"The biggest adventure you can ever take is to live

Written by
Chelsea Clinton

Illustrated by
Alexandra Boiger

PHILOMEL BOOKS

Philomel Books
an imprint of Penguin Random House LLC
375 Hudson Street
New York, NY 10014

Text copyright © 2017 by Chelsea Clinton.
Illustrations copyright © 2017 by Alexandra Boiger.

Philomel Books is a registered trademark of Penguin Random House LLC.

Library of Congress Cataloging-in-Publication Data
Names: Clinton, Chelsea, author. | Boiger, Alexandra, illustrator.
Title: She persisted : 13 American women who changed the world / written by Chelsea Clinton ; illustrated by Alexandra Boiger.
Description: New York, NY : Philomel Books, 2017.
Identifiers: LCCN 2017026184 | ISBN 9781524741723 (hardcover) | ISBN 9781524741792 (e-book)
Subjects: LCSH: Women—United States—Biography—Juvenile literature. | Women—United States—History—Juvenile literature. | Women political activists—United States—History—Juvenile literature. | Women social reformers—United States—History—Juvenile literature. | Women heroes—United States—History—Juvenile literature. | United States—Biography—Juvenile literature. | Social change—History—Juvenile literature. | Persistence—Case studies—Juvenile literature. | BISAC: JUVENILE NONFICTION / Girls & Women. | JUVENILE NONFICTION / Biography & Autobiography / Women. | JUVENILE NONFICTION / History / General.
Classification: LCC E176.8 .C57 2017 | DDC 920.72—dc23
LC record available at https://lccn.loc.gov/2017026184

Manufactured in the United States of America.
ISBN 9781524741723
10

Edited by Jill Santopolo.
Design by Ellice Lee.
Text set in ITC Kennerley.
The art was done in watercolor and ink on Fabriano paper, then edited in Photoshop.

Inspired by Senator Elizabeth Warren
and in celebration of all women who
persist every day. —C.C.

To some heroines of mine:
Coretta Scott King, Sophie Scholl,
and my mother, Berta Boiger. —A.B.

Sometimes being a girl isn't easy. At some point, someone probably will tell you no, will tell you to be quiet and may even tell you your dreams are impossible. Don't listen to them. These thirteen American women certainly did not take no for an answer.

They persisted.

HARRIET TUBMAN was born a slave, and her story could have ended there. Instead, she persisted, escaping from slavery and becoming the most famous "conductor" on the Underground Railroad. She risked her life many times to lead countless slaves to freedom, including her family, friends and strangers; every person she led to freedom arrived safely.

Once HELEN KELLER became blind and deaf as a toddler, few people thought she'd be able to learn to read, write or speak. But she persisted. Helen learned how to do all three and not only became the first person with deafblindness to graduate from college, but she used her story to help fight for more opportunities for people with disabilities, in the United States and around the world.

"One can never consent to creep when one feels an impulse to soar."

After her family fled poverty and the threat of violence in Ukraine for a new home in New York City, CLARA LEMLICH got a job working at a garment factory. She wrote that the factory's conditions made women into machines, and so **she persisted**, organizing picket lines and strikes that ultimately helped win better pay, shorter hours and safer working conditions for thousands of workers—both women and men.

NELLIE BLY became a reporter in part because a male writer had said that working women were "a monstrosity," and she wanted to prove that women could do anything. At times putting her safety at risk, she persisted throughout her career in exposing real monstrosities, pretending to be a sweatshop worker and a patient in a mental hospital to show how badly people were being treated.

"I have never written a word that did not come from my heart. I never shall."

Inspired from an early age by her brothers' childhood illnesses, VIRGINIA APGAR was determined to be a doctor, long before many girls had such dreams. Even though she qualified to be a surgeon, the male head surgeon at her hospital discouraged her because she was a woman. Nevertheless, **she persisted**, becoming an anesthesiologist and creating the Apgar score to test a newborn baby's health, which hospitals all over the world still use today.

After MARIA TALLCHIEF's family moved to California, partly to support Maria's dreams of becoming a dancer, she was teased by students in school for her Native American heritage and later was encouraged to change her last name to something that sounded Russian (since many professional dancers at the time were from Russia). She persisted, ignoring all the taunting and poor advice, to become the first great American prima ballerina.

"It never occurred
to me to say,
'It hurts to do that.'"

As a fifteen-year-old riding a bus home
from school in Montgomery, Alabama,
CLAUDETTE COLVIN was
expected to give up her seat to a white woman
just because she was African American. In her
refusal to get up, she persisted in taking a
stand for what's right, helping to inspire Rosa
Parks to make the same choice nine months
later, an act many point to as starting the
modern Civil Rights Movement.

"I knew then and I know now that, when it comes to justice, there is no easy way to get it. You can't sugarcoat it. You have to take a stand and say, 'This is not right.'"

When **RUBY BRIDGES** was in kindergarten, many schools across America, particularly in the South, still refused African American students their equal right to an education. Ruby wouldn't be treated like a second-class student, and **she persisted**, walking for weeks past angry, hateful protesters to integrate an all-white elementary school in New Orleans.

"That fateful walk to school began a journey, and we all must work together to continue moving forward."

As the first woman to serve as both a

U.S. representative and a U.S. senator,

MARGARET CHASE SMITH

could have let that fact alone be her legacy.

Instead, **she persisted** in championing women's

rights and more opportunities for women in the

military, standing up for free speech and supporting

space exploration; the head of NASA once noted

that we wouldn't have put a man on the moon

without Margaret.

"The right way is not always the popular and easy way. Standing for right when it is unpopular is a true test of moral character."

SALLY RIDE always believed women could succeed in any math or science career. Although not everyone agreed, **she persisted**, and she became the first American woman in space. But that wasn't enough for Sally. She traveled into space once more, and then created science and engineering programs specifically for girls so she could help generations of young women achieve their dreams, too—both on Earth and in outer space.

"Young girls need to see role models in whatever careers they may choose, just so they can picture themselves doing those jobs someday.

You can't be what you can't see."

When, as a kid,

FLORENCE GRIFFITH JOYNER

visited her father in the Mojave Desert, he would
urge her to run faster and faster—to run as fast as a
jackrabbit. Even when she had to leave college to help
support her family, **she persisted** in her training on
the track, then went back to school and got faster and
faster; her unbroken world records in the 100-meter and
200-meter sprints set at the 1988 Summer Olympics
mean she is still the fastest woman ever.

"When anyone tells me I can't do anything . . .

OPRAH WINFREY's grandmother expected Oprah to follow in her footsteps and become a maid. Oprah knew, even as a little girl, that her dreams would take her somewhere else. She persisted in turning those dreams into her reality and became a media superstar, working in movies, books, magazines, theater and, most of all, television, where *The Oprah Winfrey Show* remains the highest-rated talk show of all time.

"The biggest adventure you can ever take

is to live the life of your dreams."

justicia ~ justice
juez ~ judge
ley ~ law

Watching fictional judges on television inspired
SONIA SOTOMAYOR to want to
be a real-life judge when she grew up. She knew
she'd have to speak English as well as she spoke
Spanish, study hard in school and manage her
diabetes before she could one day wear a judge's robe
with a gavel in hand. She persisted, eventually
becoming a Supreme Court justice and the first-ever
Latina to sit on America's highest court.

"I have never had to
face anything that could
overwhelm the native optimism
and stubborn perseverance
I was blessed with."

So, if anyone ever tells you no,

if anyone ever says your voice isn't important

or your dreams are too big,

remember these women.

They persisted and so should you.